Martin Luther's Little Instruction Book

A Classic Treasury of
Timeless Wisdom and Reflection

Tulsa, Oklahoma

Martin Luther's Little Instruction Book:
A Classic Treasury of Timeless Wisdom and Reflection
ISBN 1-56292-039-1
Copyright © 1996 by Honor Books, Inc.
P.O. Box 55388
Tulsa, Oklahoma 74155

INTRODUCTION

Over four hundred years ago, a German monk and professor of theology named Martin Luther quietly challenged the widespread practice of buying your way into heaven through the purchase of indulgences. (An indulgence was being forgiven and absolved of any punishment for a sin from a church representative.) His motivation came from the biblical truth that to inherit eternal life with God, "the just shall live by faith." Little did he realize his teachings would begin the largest Christian movement in the world — Protestantism.

Before coming to this understanding, Luther had remained perplexed by his inability to be holy enough for God to love. This drove him to a an in-depth study of the Bible, where he discovered that only the work of Jesus Christ on the cross paid the price for his sins. He realized that only through faith in Jesus as his Lord and Savior would he become a child of God, a true Christian. Rather than trusting in his good deeds, he simply believed in Jesus and received eternal life.

Luther's relevation of the grace of God, which opposed the manmade religious traditions of his time, has left an undeniable mark on our civilization. Known as the father of the Reformation, Martin Luther was a multi-faceted character who could be both tenderhearted and generous, as well as confrontational and feisty. He greatly enjoyed God's earthly pleasures — food and drink, music and humor — and after being a monk he particularly appreciated married life.

In his engaging style, Luther addressed many issues that are strikingly relevant today. The selections in this small volume give you a sample of his wit and wisdom, his giant stature, and the simple humanness of a man who knew he was loved by God.

Note: All quotes are Martin Luther unless indicated otherwise.

⌒ YES AND AMEN ⌒

"Faith is the 'yes' of the heart, a conviction
on which one stakes one's life."

DID YOU KNOW?

Hans Luder, (later changed to Luther), of peasant stock,
married Margaretta Lindemann, of a middle class family.
They wanted their son, Martin, to become a lawyer.
He initially disappointed them by becoming a monk.

THE KEY TO HIS CONVERSION

"When by the Spirit of God, I understood these words, 'The just shall live by faith,' I felt born again like a new man. I entered through the open doors into the very Paradise of God!"

———

"The just shall live by faith."

ROMANS 1:17

BELIEVING THOUGH NOT SEEING

"[It is] astounding that I should believe him to be the Son of God who is suspended on the cross, whom I have never seen, with whom I have never become acquainted."

"Whom having not seen, ye love; in whom, though now ye see him not, yet believing, ye rejoice with joy unspeakable and full of glory."

1 PETER 1:8

∼ FAITH COMES ∼ FROM GOD

"Your faith comes from Him, not from you. And everything that works faith within you comes from Him and not from you."

MAKING SOMETHING OUT OF NOTHING

"God creates out of nothing.
Therefore, until a man is nothing,
God can make nothing out of him."

PREACHING TO THE MAIDS AND BABES

"When I preach I regard neither doctors nor magistrates, of whom I have above forty in my congregation; I have all my eyes on the servant maids and on the children. And if the learned men are not well pleased with what they hear, well, the door is open."

BEGIN WHEN YOU'RE YOUNG

"When I was young, I read the Bible over and over and over again, and was so perfectly acquainted with it, that I could, in an instant, have pointed to any verse that might have been mentioned."

◠ NO SUCH THING ◠ AS PERFECT

"Farewell to those who want an entirely pure and purified church. This is plainly wanting no church at all."

SING TO GOD!

"The devil should not be allowed to keep all the best tunes for himself."

_____

"_I will praise the name of God with a song, and will magnify him with thanksgiving._"

PSALM 69:30

ACCEPT GOD'S CALL

"Be content in the calling God has placed you. I have not learned it yet."

_____

"But now hath God set the members every one of them in the body, as it hath pleased Him."

1 CORINTHIANS 12:18

MARITAL BLISS

"To have peace and love in a marriage is a gift that is next to the knowledge of the gospel."

THE LAW NEEDS GRACE

"Without grace the Law kills a man and increases sin."

"But where sin abounded, grace did much more abound."

ROMANS 5:20

DID YOU KNOW?

Before he became a friar, Luther was
well on his way to becoming a lawyer.
He had earned both his bachelor's and master's
degrees in the shortest time possible.

⤙ BEARING ⤚
OTHERS' FAULTS

"The love toward our neighbors must be like the pure and chaste love between bride and bridegroom, where all faults are connived at [overlooked] and borne with, and only the virtues regarded."

AN ASTONISHING DEATH

"The greatest wonder ever on earth is, that the Son of God died the shameful death of the cross. It is astonishing, that the Father should say to his only Son, who by nature is God: Go, let them hang thee on the gallows."

"Yet it was the Lord's will to crush him and cause him to suffer....For he bore the sin of many, and made intercession for the transgressors.

ISAIAH 53:10,12

KEEP THE WORD PURE

"No greater mischief can happen to a Christian people, than to have God's word taken from them, or falsified, so that they no longer have it pure and clear."

TRUTH WITH ABILITY

"All laws and philosophy merely tell us what should be done, but they do not provide the strength to do it."

———

"For when we were yet without strength, in due time Christ died for the ungodly."

ROMANS 5:6

THE ONLY COMFORTER

"Without Christ no one can comfort himself."

⌒ THE SPIRIT AND ⌒ THE WORD AGREE

"Whenever a man reads the Word of God, the Holy Spirit is speaking to him."

DID YOU KNOW?

While walking back to law school in 1505,
Luther encountered a frightening thunderstorm.
Because he knew he was not prepared to die,
he cried out in fear, "Help me, St. Anna!
I will become a monk!" He kept his vow.

SATAN A PREACHER?

"The devil, too, can quote Scripture. But his use of Scripture is defective. He does not quote it completely but only so much of it as serves his purpose. The rest he silently omits."

THE BUILDING OF GOD

"We do not know how our Lord God is preparing His structure. We see only the scaffolding of stakes and ropes.... But in the future life we shall see the structure and building of God and, filled with wonder,...we shall rejoice at having endured the trials."

"...Christ loved the church and gave himself up for her to make her holy...without stain or wrinkle or any other blemish, but holy and blameless."

EPHESIANS 5:25-27

⟨ SCRIPTURE ABOVE ⟩ OUR PROOF

"An orthodox person gives the glory to God and does not doubt that everything has been put down well and correctly in Scripture, even though he may not know how to prove everything."

HUMAN NATURE

"Man is by nature unable to want God to be God. Indeed he himself wants to be God, and does not want God to be God."

GOVERNMENT BEGINS IN THE HOME

"If obedience is not rendered in the homes, we shall never have a whole city, country, principality, or kingdom well governed."

THE LEAST GIFT

"Wealth is the smallest thing on earth, the least gift that God has bestowed on mankind."

THE PURPOSE OF MINISTRY

"It is the work and the glory of the ministry to make real saints out of sinners, living souls out of the dead, saved souls out of the damned, children of God out of servants of the devil."

DID YOU KNOW?

When Luther became a priest and celebrated
his first Mass, in 1507, he trembled so much
he nearly dropped the bread and the wine.
He became so terrified of the presence of Christ
in the sacrament that he tried to run from the altar.

 LESSONS OF LOVE

"Love teaches very readily how to conduct yourself well in all situations; and without it nothing whatever can be satisfactorily taught."

⌒ LIVING "WORD" ⌒
PERFECT

"We should not consider the slightest error against the Word of God unimportant."

THE WORLD'S EMPTY PROMISES

"The world promises great things but delivers few. It acts like hosts who give their guests too little and console them with empty words."

⌒ THE DIVINE ⌒
ABOVE THE HUMAN

"The truth is mightier than eloquence, the Spirit greater than genius, faith more than education."

⤨ UNSEALING ⤪
THE LETTER

"The New Testament is nothing but a revelation of the Old Testament, as if one were in possession of a sealed letter and then later on opened it."

FLYING FRIED CHICKEN

"He does not want me to sit at home, to loaf, to commit matters to God, and to wait till a fried chicken flies into my mouth. That would be tempting God."

———

"Therefore my beloved brethren, be ye steadfast, unmoveable, always abounding in the work of the Lord.

1 CORINTHIANS 15:58

⌒ HIGH-SPIRITED ⌒ MINISTERS

"He must be of a high and great spirit that undertakes to serve the people in body and soul, for he must suffer the utmost danger and unthankfulness."

DID YOU KNOW?

Luther and his wife Katie had six children.
Two of them died by the age of 14.

A LOVE-HATE RELATION-SHIP

"God loves and hates temptations. He loves them when they provoke us to pray to Him and trust in Him; He hates them when we despair because of them."

The testing of your faith develops perseverance. Perseverance must finish its work so that you may be mature and complete, not lacking anything.

JAMES 1:3,4 NIV

REASON FALLS SHORT

"Reason is…a beautiful light. But it cannot [alone]…find the path that will lead from sin and from death to righteousness and to life; it remains in darkness."

But of him are ye in Christ Jesus, who of God is made unto us wisdom, and righteousness, and sanctification, and redemption.

1 CORINTHIANS 1:30

LOVE LOOKS LIKE GOD

"The more a person loves, the closer he approaches the image of God."

HOPE FOR THE BEST

"In all matters we should hope and pray for the best; nevertheless, we should be prepared for the worst."

"Hope deferred makes the heart sick, but a longing fulfilled is a tree of life."

PROVERBS 13:12 NIV

A CHEERFUL CREATION

"God wants us to be cheerful, and He hates sadness. For had He wanted us to be sad, He would not have given us the sun, the moon, and the various fruits of the earth. All these He gave for our good cheer."

"Sing O heavens; and be joyful, O earth; and break forth into singing, O mountains: for the Lord hath comforted his people, and will have mercy upon his afflicted."

ISAIAH 49:13

⤚ THE PERFECT ⤙ WEDDING RING

"Faith is the wedding ring with which we have pledged ourselves to Christ."

CENTRAL DOCTRINE

"Now the article of justification, which is our sole defense, not only against all the force and craft of man, but also against the gates of hell, is this: that by faith only in Christ, and without works, we are pronounced righteous and saved."

"For by grace are ye saved through faith; and that not of yourselves: it is the gift of God: Not of works, lest any man should boast."

EPHESIANS 2:8,9

THE TREASURE OF EDUCATION

"You parents cannot prepare a more dependable treasure for your children than an education in the liberal arts. House and home burn down and disappear, but an education is easy to carry off."

"Whoever gives heed to instruction prospers."

PROVERBS 16:20 NIV

⟨ MASQUERADING ⟩ AS VIRTUE

"These two sins, hatred and pride, deck and trim themselves out, as the devil clothed himself, in the Godhead. Hatred will be godlike; pride will be truth."

PRATTLE AND PREACH

"Since we are preaching to children, we must also prattle with them."

[*prattle*—to speak in a childish way.]

❧ STOP AND WEAR OUT ❧

"If I rest, I rust."

HUMILITY'S GREATEST EXAMPLE

"'Tis a high example, that he so deeply humbled himself and suffered, who created the whole world, heaven and earth."

"*Who being in the form of God...took upon him the form of a servant, and was made in the likeness of men,....he humbled himself and became obedient unto death, even the death of the cross.*"

PHILIPPIANS 2:6-8

⌒ SECOND ONLY ⌒
TO THE HOLY GHOST

"In domestic affairs I defer to [my wife] Katie.
Otherwise, I am led by the Holy Ghost."

THE PLAGUE OF IDLENESS

"For to be full and idle is the greatest plague on earth; it is the trouble whence all other plagues come."

"If a man is lazy, the rafters sag; if his hands are idle, the house leaks."

ECCLESIASTES 10:18 NIV

MUSIC — GOD'S GIFT

"I have no use for cranks who despise music, because it is a gift of God. Next after theology, I give to music the highest place and the greatest honor."

DID YOU KNOW?

Luther took on a disguise and hid in Wartburg Castle from Roman Catholic authorities from 1520-21. While there he let his hair and beard grow, dressed as a soldier and was known as "Knight George."

A PRICKLY SITUATION

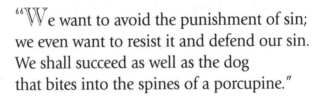

"We want to avoid the punishment of sin;
we even want to resist it and defend our sin.
We shall succeed as well as the dog
that bites into the spines of a porcupine."

 AN EMPIRE FOR A ROSE

"If a man could make a single rose, an empire should be given him. But, because of their commonness, innumerable gifts of God are not appreciated."

❧ WHAT CAN WE GIVE GOD?

"We cannot give God anything; for everything is already His, and all we have comes from Him. We can only give Him praise, thanks and honor."

⌒ HOW TO ⌒
RECEIVE GRACE

"Certain it is that man must completely despair of himself in order to become fit to receive the grace of Christ."

A FEW GOOD BOOKS

"A student who does not want his labor wasted must so read and reread some good writer that the author is changed, as it were, into his flesh and blood. For a great variety of reading confuses and does not teach."

SILENCE YOUR TONGUE

"Men should think it over well
and not obey anger which is hasty
and has the word on the tongue
and not in the heart."

_____

*"The discretion of a man deferreth
his anger; and it is his glory to
pass over a transgression."*

PROVERBS 19:11

ENDING WELL

"God orders us to work and to do whatever our calling requires. Therefore he who looks to his calling and continues to work diligently, even if good fortune is against him and success fails to come for a while, is bound to fare well in the end."

"And let us not be weary in well doing: for in due season we shall reap, if we faint not."

GALATIANS 6:9

⇌ THE CARPENTER ⇌
AND HIS WOOD

"He is the Carpenter, and we are the wood. His handiwork is the dear, the holy cross, which is bound to follow upon the teaching of the Gospel. He plies His tools and works on us, planes and carves us, in order to kill the old man within us."

DID YOU KNOW?

Though only a legend, the story of Luther hurling an inkwell at the devil, has a connection to truth. Luther regularly engaged in intense spiritual warfare as he furthered the Reformation.

⌒ LIKE FATHER, ⌒
LIKE SON?

"Proud jackasses develop out of the sons of heroes who boast of the virtue of their fathers but make no effort to imitate it, dreaming instead that they, too, are heroes because they were born of heroes."

RESTLESS PURSUITS

"The flesh is forever moving from present possessions to future ones. It loses the former in the pursuit of the latter and thus deprives itself of the use of both."

⌒ A HUNDRED ⌒ THOUSAND EXCUSES

"When I would speak and pray to God by myself a hundred thousand hindrances at once intervene before I get at it. Then the devil can throw all sorts of reasons for delay into my path."

HIS LIGHT BURDEN

There is no work on earth easier than the true service of God; he loads us with no heavy burdens, but only asks that we believe in him and preach of him.

"My yoke is easy, and my burden is light."

MATTHEW 11:28

A WIFE — GOD'S GIFT

"A good wife is not found accidentally and without divine guidance. On the contrary, she is a gift of God and does not come, as the heathen imagine, in answer to our planning and judging."

"Houses and wealth are inherited from parents, but a prudent wife is from the Lord."

PROVERBS 19:14 NIV

A PRAYER FOR STRENGTH

"Behold, Lord, here is an empty cask that needs to be filled. My Lord, fill it. I am weak in faith, strengthen me. I am cold in love; warm me and fill me with fire that my love may flow out over my neighbor."

"God divided the hand into fingers so that money would slip through."

GIVING GENEROUSLY

"Give, and it will be given to you...For whatever measure you deal out to others, it will be dealt to you in return."

LUKE 6:38 NASB

A POSITION OF HONOR

"No power on earth is so noble and so great as that of parents."

DID YOU KNOW?

The hymn, "A Mighty Fortress is our God,"
was set to the tune of a common tavern song.

WORTHLESS RESERVES

"What sort of faith is that which trusts in God when all the while you feel and know that you have provisions in reserve by which you are able to help yourself?"

⌒ WORDS THAT ⌒
DIFFER GREATLY

"We must make a great difference between God's Word and the word of man. A man's word is a little sound, that flies into the air, and soon vanishes; but the Word of God is greater than heaven and earth."

CHILDREN
—
GOD'S CREATION

"Daily learn the article of divine creation by looking at your children and offspring, who stand before you...Here you may behold the providence of God, who created them out of nothing."

"Lo, children are an heritage from the Lord: and the fruit of the womb is his reward."

PSALM 127:3

THE LIVING WORD

"The Bible is alive, it speaks to me; it has feet,
it runs after me; it has hands, it lays hold of me."

⌒ SOON ⌒
FORGOTTEN HERE

"As all people feel they must die, each seeks immortality here on earth, that he may be had in everlasting remembrance."

⌒ WATCHING ⌒ OVER CHILDREN

"The dear angels are not so proud as we human beings are. They walk in obedience to God, serve mankind, and take care of little children. How could they perform a more insignificant work than taking care of children day and night?"

DEFENDING THE FAITH

"Here stand I. I can do no other. God help me. Amen."

(Defense before the Diet of Worms, 1521, where clergymen challenged Luther's teachings were heresy.)

WHOM WILL YOU SERVE?

"Whatever your heart clings to and confides in, that is really your God."

⌒ KEEPING THE ⌒ WOLVES AT BAY

"An upright shepherd and minister must improve his flock by edification, and also resist and defend it; otherwise, if resisting be absent, the wolf devours the sheep."

DID YOU KNOW?

Like many Christians of today, Luther saw many
of Daniel's prophecies fulfilled in his day, which caused
him to believe the return of Jesus Christ was imminent.

JUSTIFIED FOR WORKS

"He who is justified performs good works; for this is the meaning of Scripture: Justification precedes good works, and works are performed by those who are justified."

"For we are his workmanship, created in Christ Jesus unto good works, which God hath before ordained that we should walk in them."

EPHESIANS 2:10

⌒ DEVILS ON THE ROOF ⌒

"If I heard that as many devils would set on me in Worms as there are tiles on the roofs, I should none the less have ridden there."

(The city of Worms, Germany, was where Luther's teachings were challenged as heresy.)

⌒ GOD'S ⌒
REPRESENTATIVES

"We must train young people to look upon their parents as God's representatives and to remember that even though they are lowly, poor, frail, and peculiar, they are still the father and mother whom God gave them."

⌒ SPIRITUAL PRIDE ⌒

"Reason cannot break itself of this habit: if it find itself favored by God before others, it must turn up its nose at those who do not enjoy such favor."

BLINDED BY THE LIGHT

"Blessed is he who delights in [the Word of God] and gladly see this light, for it loves to shine. But moles and bats, that is, the people of the world, do not like it."

DID YOU KNOW?

Luther enjoyed playing the lute. He also challenged tradition by encouraging congregational hymn singing, which had formerly been reserved for the choir.

⌒ TOO VAST ⌒ TO UNDERSTAND

"I shall need to have been dead several years before I shall thoroughly understand the meaning of creation and the omnipotence of God."

A PENITENT HEART

"A penitent heart is a rare thing and a great grace; one cannot produce it by thinking about sin and hell. Only the Holy Spirit can impart it."

"Search me, O God, and know my heart: try me, and know my thoughts: And see if there be any wicked way in me, and lead me in the way everlasting."

PSALM 139:24

THE BARKING DOG OF REGRET

"Regret, the little black dog of a belated repentance, does not stop barking and biting the conscience, even though you know that your sins are forgiven."

BELIEVE ON THE SON!

"It is the will and pleasure of the Father that he who sees the Son and believes on Him have eternal life. Would to God this fact would sink into the heart! If only people would think what this means!"

～ THE GREATEST ～ PURIFIER

"A fiery shield is God's Word; of more substance and purer than gold, which, tried in the fire, loses nought of its substance."

FREEDOM TO SERVE

"A Christian is a free lord of all and subject to no one. A Christian is a ministering servant of all and subject to everyone."

LOVING THE RASCALS

"Our Lord God must be a pious man to be able to love rascals. I can't do it and yet I am a rascal myself."

⌒ HE BORE ⌒
OUR PUNISHMENT

"Christ is the One who stepped into the place of our sinful nature, loaded upon Himself, and appeased for us all, the wrath of God which we had deserved by all our works."

FREE WILL IS SELF WILL

"I wish that the expression "free will" had never been invented. It is not recorded in Scripture either and should more justly be called self-will, which is worthless."

NO MORE BOOKS

"I would indeed consent to have all my books perish; for I have sought nothing with them but to bring to light Holy Scripture and the divine truth."

WHAT YOU LOSE, YOU GIVE

"For whatever your injury and loss of temporal possessions may be, they are, in these circumstances, sacrifices offered to Christ Himself."

"And everyone who has left houses or brothers or sisters or father or mother or children or fields for my sake will receive a hundred times as much and will inherit eternal life."

MATTHEW 19:29 NIV

A PURE HEART

"No one is better prepared for Judgment Day than the person who longs to be without sin."

"Create in me a clean heart, O God; and renew a right spirit within me."

PSALM 51:10

THE GREATEST OF THESE IS...

"Patience, chasteness, moderation, etc. are fine virtues, too; but they are trivial when compared with love, which includes all other virtues and brings them in its train."

"If I give all I possess to the poor and surrender my body to the flames, but have not love, I gain nothing."

1 CORINTHIANS 13:3 NIV

UNEXPECTED REWARDS

"It is impossible that reward should not follow when we seek God in a purely selfless spirit, without any expectation of reward and advantage."

___

"He is a rewarder of them that diligently seek him."

HEBREWS 11:6

WRATH AND MERCY

"The wrath of God is real, not fictitious, not a jest. If it were false, then mercy would be fictitious; for as the wrath, so the mercy which forgives..."

CRAWLING TOWARD HEAVEN

"Why, then, am I, when my soul's salvation is concerned, so sluggish and sleepy that God must drag me to it by the very hair? Why, I ought to spit at myself for not even crawling to heaven while those folk rush and run to hell the way they do."

DID YOU KNOW?

Though Luther is considered one of history's
greatest preachers, he was discouraged
with the progress of his congregation, and
even refused to preach for a while.

WHEN WORK IS SIN

"To want to merit grace by works which precede faith is to want to appease God by sins."

⟨ HANDLING ⟩ POSSESSIONS

"Possessions are not given that we may rely on them and glory in them...but that we may use and enjoy them and share them with others...Our possessions should be in our hands, not in our hearts."

TO GOSSIPS AND SLANDERERS

"If you were his friend, you would keep silent and not circulate the misfortune of your neighbor with such pleasure and delight. In fact, you would convert your displeasure into pity and mercy."

———

"It is the glory of God to conceal a matter."

PROVERBS 25:2 NIV

A BIG SNOWBALL

"A lie is like a snowball. The longer it is rolled on the ground, the larger it becomes."

~ THE DANGER OF PRIDE ~

"It is a particularly perilous task not to turn proud but to remain humble if God graces a person with outstanding, splendid talents."

～ SECRET ～
OF CONTENTMENT

"Now he who…knows that we are all equal in Christ goes about his work with delight and is not concerned even though for this short time here on earth he is in more modest circumstances and in a lowlier position than another."

❧ KNOWING ❧
BY EXPERIENCE

"No one understands Scripture unless it is brought home to him, that is, unless he experiences it."

FAITH AND LOVE WORKING TOGETHER

"Faith receives the good works of Christ; love does good works for the neighbor."

UNITY AT THE EXPENSE OF THE WORD

"Accursed be the love and the harmony for the preservation of which men endanger the Word of God."

FOUNDATIONAL DOCTRINES

"The litany of litanies is the Lord's Prayer.
The learning of the learned is the Ten Commandments.
The virtue of the virtuous is the Apostles Creed...
These three make a person perfect an absolute in thought, word, and deed; that is they nourish and bring to the highest perfection the mind, tongue, and body."

⌒ DON'T WAIT TO PRAY! ⌒

"Guard yourself carefully against those false, deluding ideas which tell you, *Wait a little while. I will pray in an hour; first I must attend to this or that.*"

DID YOU KNOW?

Luther raised such controversy that it was rumored
he was the product of a liaison between his mother and
the Devil. At the Diet of Worms he was condemned as
a "demon in the appearance of a man."

PEACE FROM HIS MERITS

"The way of peace is to believe without merits, nay, despite the greatest demerits simply to rely on the mercy of the Lord, just as the psalm bids us do: 'Cast thy burden upon the Lord.'"

"Cast thy burden upon the Lord, and he shall sustain thee: he shall never suffer the righteous to be moved."

PSALM 55:22

A HEALTHY FEAR

"Being afraid of God is different from fearing God. The fear of God is a fruit of love, but being afraid of Him is the seed of hatred."

_____

"The fear of the Lord is the beginning of knowledge: but fools despise wisdom and instruction.

PROVERBS 1:7

FAITH, NO DOUBT

"We must constantly fight against doubt and unbelief, so great and difficult a matter is faith."

～ A BAD DOG ～
ON A CHAIN

"[The devil] can do no more than a bad dog on a chain, which may bark, run here and there, and tear at the chain. But because it is tied and you avoid it, it cannot bite you."

WELCOMING DEATH

"Christians look at [death] as a journey and departure out of this misery and vale of tears (where the devil is prince and god) into yonder life, where there will be inexpressible and glorious joy and eternal blessedness."

A BELIEVER'S DUTY

"To serve God properly means that everyone stay in his calling, however humble it may be, and first heed the Word of God in church, then the word of the government, superiors, or parents, and then live accordingly."

UNJUST TO COMPLAIN

"It ill becomes a Christian to complain and clamor much about injustice done to him."

"The Lord shall fight for you, and ye shall hold your peace."

EXODUS 14:14

FUSSING, OR HAVING FAITH?

"We should not become impatient but should learn to watch, wait, and continue steadfast in faith; for we see what people are like when they become impatient, how they fuss and fume and carry on. They only hinder their own praying and praising."

⌒ PRACTICE ⌒
YOUR PREACHING

"God grant us all to live as we teach and to practice what we preach."

DID YOU KNOW?

Luther committed to memory much of the Bible, including the Old Testament.

CARELESS WORK

"We should indeed work, but we should let God have the care. After all, our worrying gets us nowhere. Meanwhile we might have done much good, but our care has kept us from it."

"Casting all your care upon him; for he careth for you."
1 PETER 5:7

RIGHT DOCTRINE ESSENTIAL

"It is true, where the doctrine is not right, it is impossible for the life to be right and good; for life is fathered and fashioned by doctrine."

"The entrance of thy words giveth light; it giveth understanding unto the simple."
PSALM 119:130

DO NOT CRUSH A CHILD

"Children are not to be rebuked or beaten, but that they are to be chastised in love; but parents are not to vent their furious temper on them… For when the spirit has been cowed, one is of no use for anything."

"And fathers, do not provoke your children to anger; but bring them up in the discipline and instruction of the Lord."

EPHESIANS 6:4 NASB

CHOOSING A WIFE

"Ask God to give you a good, pious girl, with whom you spend your life in mutual love For sex [alone] establishes nothing…there must also be agreement in values and character."

"Can two walk together, except they be agreed?"

AMOS 3:3

ANGELS AT OUR SIDE

"You should be certain that angels are protecting you when you go to sleep, yea, that they are protecting you also in all your business, whether you enter your home or leave your home."

"Are not all angels ministering spirits sent to serve those who will inherit salvation?"

HEBREWS 1:14 NIV

⌢ WHERE THERE ⌢ IS SMOKE

"Just as there is no fire without heat and smoke, so there is no faith without love."

OVERCOMING CIRCUMSTANCES

"If I really recognize my blessings, my heart laughs; and if He sends me misfortune, trouble, and danger, I take to thanking Him and say: God be forever praised for chastising me in this way."

"I have learned the secret of being content in any and every situation, whether well fed or hungry, whether living in plenty or in want."

PHILIPPIANS 4:12 NIV

⌒ LIFE'S UPS ⌒ AND DOWNS

"How is God to arrange our life? Good days we cannot bear; evil days we cannot endure. If He gives us wealth, we strut about; if He gives us poverty, we despair. It would be best to hurry us under ground with the spade."

DID YOU KNOW?

By the end of his life, Martin Luther wrote over 60,000 pages, yet he hoped that his books would disappear and only the Holy Scriptures be read.

THE EASIEST THING IN THE WORLD

"Nothing is easier than sinning."

⌒ COMFORTED ⌒
BEYOND OUR SENSES

"The comfort men give consists in external, visible help, which one can grasp, see, and feel. The comfort God gives consists only in the Word and promise, without seeing, hearing, or feeling."

⌒ TRIALS ⌒ ARE BENEFICIAL

"One Christian who has been tried is worth a hundred who have not been tried, for the blessing of God grows in trials. He who has experienced them can teach, comfort, and advise many in bodily and spiritual matters."

⇒ THE HOLY SPIRIT'S ⇐
BEST SELLER

"The Bible is the special, very own Book, Writing, and Word of the Holy Spirit."

BLESSED DEPARTURE

"The hour of our death is a heavenly gift for which we should constantly ask God and daily prepare ourselves so that...we look forward to our departure and our gain with pious longing."

"For me to live is Christ and die is gain."

PHILIPPIANS 1:21 NIV

DID YOU KNOW?

There are approximately 60 million Lutherans around the world.

THE BURDEN OF PROSPERITY

"When things are going well, a man cannot control himself by means of his own powers; he becomes presumptuous, prides himself on his wealth and good fortune, and passes away."

⌒ THE ONGOING ⌒ ARGUMENT

"Think of all the squabbles Adam and Eve must have had in the course of their nine hundred years. Eve would say, 'You ate the apple,' and Adam would retort, 'You gave it to me.'"

LOVING ANTICIPATION

"Let the wife make her husband glad to come home and let him make her sorry he leaves."

TWO THINGS — ALONE

"Every man must do two things alone; he must do his own believing and his own dying."

RANKS OF THE ENEMY

"They are small devils that tempt with lasciviousness and avarice; higher spirits tempt with unbelief, and despair, and heresy."

For we wrestle not against flesh and blood, but against principalities, against powers, against the rulers of the darkness of this world, against spiritual wickedness in high places.

EPHESIANS 6:12

SPRING RISES AGAIN

"Our Lord has written the promise of the resurrection, not in books alone, but in every leaf of springtime."

⤜ PRAYER STOKES ⤠ THE FIRE

"If I should neglect prayer but a single day, I should lose a great deal of the fire of faith."

∼ PRAYER ∼
OUR LIFEBLOOD

"To be a Christian without prayer is no more possible than to be alive without breathing."

THE FOOLS WHO ARE WISE

"It is characteristic of a Christian to have the greatest strength in the greatest weakness and the greatest wisdom in the greatest foolishness."

"For when I am weak, then I am strong."
2 CORINTHIANS 12:10 NIV

GOD LOVES LAUGHTER

"It is pleasing to God whenever you rejoice or laugh from the bottom of your heart."

Even though you do not see him now, you are filled with an inexpressible and glorious joy.

1 PETER 1:8 NIV

A MIGHTY FORTRESS IS OUR GOD

"A mighty fortress is our God,
A bulwark never failing;
Our helper He, amid the flood
Of mortal ills prevailing.
For still our ancient foe
Doth seek to work us woe;
His craft and power are great,
And, armed with cruel hate,
On earth is not his equal."

A MIGHTY FORTRESS
(v.2)

"Did we in our own strength confide,
Our striving would be losing,
Were not the right Man on our side,
The Man of God's own choosing.
Dost ask who that may be?
Christ Jesus, it is He;
Lord Sabaoth His name,
From age to age the same,
And He must win the battle."

A MIGHTY FORTRESS
(v.3)

"And though this world, with devils filled,
Should threaten to undo us,
We will not fear, for God hath willed
His truth to triumph through us.
The prince of darkness grim
We tremble not for him;
His rage we can endure,
For lo! his doom is sure,
One little word shall fell him."

⪢ A MIGHTY FORTRESS ⪡
(v.4)

"That word above all earthly powers
No thanks to them abideth;
The Spirit and the gifts are ours
Through Him who with us sideth.
Let goods and kindred go,
This mortal life also;
the body they may kill:
God's truth abideth still,
His kingdom is forever."

Additional copies of this book and other
portable book titles from **Honor Books**
are available at your local bookstore:

Dwight L. Moody's Little Instruction Book

John Wesley's Little Instruction Book

Larry Burkett's Little Instruction Book

God's Little Instruction Book (series)